Mark Humphries and Evan Williams a[re]
resident satirists on the ABC's *7.30*. They
previously created satirical sketches for SBS's
*The Feed* and the ABC's *The Roast*. Neither of
these shows were about food. In 2018, Prime
Minister Scott Morrison wrote of one of their
sketches 'Love your work. Had a good laugh'. He's
been a bit more quiet lately.

Mark's writing has appeared in *The Guardian*
and the *Sun-Herald*. As a presenter, Mark has
guest-hosted 'Talking Pictures' on the ABC's
*Insiders* and was the host of the Network 10 quiz
show *Pointless*. He was also the winner of *Celebrity
Mastermind* but never likes to bring it up.

Evan's writing has appeared in the *New Yorker*,
*McSweeney's*, the *Sydney Morning Herald*, *The
Guardian*, *The Monthly* and *The Mini Whiteboard
on the Fridge Where he Writes the Grocery List*.

## Writers in the On Series

Fleur Anderson

Gay Bilson

John Birmingham

Chris Bowen

Julian Burnside

Paul Daley

Blanche d'Alpuget

Glyn Davis

Robert Dessaix

Juliana Engberg

Sarah Ferguson

Nikki Gemmell

Stan Grant

Germaine Greer

Sarah Hanson-Young

Jonathan Holmes

Daisy Jeffrey

Susan Johnson

Malcolm Knox

Barrie Kosky

David Malouf

Paula Matthewson

Sally McManus

Rick Morton

Katharine Murphy

Dorothy Porter

Leigh Sales

Mark Scott

Tory Shepherd

Annika Smethurst

Tim Soutphommasane

David Speers

Natasha Stott Despoja

Anne Summers

Tony Wheeler

Ashleigh Wilson

Elisabeth Wynhausen

# Mark Humphries & Evan Williams

# On Politics

*and stuff*

hachette
AUSTRALIA

**hachette**
AUSTRALIA

Published in Australia and New Zealand in 2021
by Hachette Australia
(an imprint of Hachette Australia Pty Limited)
Level 17, 207 Kent Street, Sydney NSW 2000
www.hachette.com.au

10 9 8 7 6 5 4 3 2 1

A catalogue record for this
book is available from the
National Library of Australia

ISBN: 978 0 7336 4656 0 (paperback)

Text design by Alice Graphics
Typeset by Kirby Jones
Back cover and page i author photographs by Chloe Angelo
Cover by Luke Causby/Blue Cork
Printed and bound in Australia by McPherson's Printing Group

*'It's a hell of a town'*

– Walter Burley Griffin on New York City

When one embarks on writing a book about Australian politics, one finds there is no better starting point than Canberra. Canberra is a planned city. And if the idea was to create an utterly unremarkable urban environment, then you have to tip your hat. Yes, Canberra was once known for legal pornography and legal fireworks, but now it's so much less than that, being only the home of Australian politics.

Passing through the city, it's impossible not to think of the many historic political figures who once navigated these relentless roundabouts. Unfortunately, it's also impossible to remember their names. Robert Mumps? Is that one? Bill Chipley? No, that's not right. Who was the guy who ate the onion again? Don't worry, you can google it later. For now, just take in the atmosphere.

Canberra, with her frosty mornings allowing the outlines of middle-aged men's nipples to bloom beneath their identical crisp white shirts. Canberra, with her litres of sweat trapped in the lycra of cycling middle-aged men, enough to perhaps hydrate a sizable village. Canberra, O Canberra. Thank you for being there when we needed some place roughly equidistant between Sydney and Melbourne.

Of course, talk of this city prompts the question every aspiring politician is trying to answer: How do you *get* to Canberra? Yes, Murrays Coaches provides services departing Sydney's Central Station hourly, but we're speaking metaphorically. That said, you will need to get there somehow, and you could do worse than the team at Murrays. Look, we're not here to 'sell' you on Murrays, but if you were so inclined, use the promo code ONPOLITICS at checkout for a surprisingly generous discount.

But before you buy your ticket, you should know that the Canberra life is not for everyone. In fact, many politicians find it so dull they eventually break down in tears and claim that they want to 'spend more time with their family'. On the other hand, apparently there are a few interesting restaurants popping up in Canberra these days, so, swings and roundabouts. Oh so many roundabouts.

But if one decides that the Canberra life is the one for one, then one will be embarking on one hell of a journey.[1] With nothing more than a Murrays ticket in one hand, a briefcase full of bland talking points in the other, and a void in your heart that can only be filled by the validation of the masses, you might just have what it takes to make it in the town where the nation's politicians reluctantly come to work and play. (If you can define sitting around

---

1  Authors' note: After a robust discussion with Hachette's copyeditor, we have generously agreed to remove five 'one's from this sentence.

drinking single vineyard cabernet sauvignon and coldly dissecting the political minutiae of the day as 'play'.)

> *'I did but see her passing by,*
> *and yet I love her till I die'*
>
> – Robert Menzies on his first sighting of a Murrays coach

There are a handful of famous addresses in politics. 1600 Pennsylvania Avenue, 10 Downing Street and, of course, 5 Adelaide Avenue, Deakin. If you enter this address into your preferred search engine, you'll stumble upon the kind of historic home you'd quickly scroll past on an Airbnb search of Canberra properties. But for many politicians, this Dijon mustard-coloured building called The Lodge is the place they wish they could call home. O, what they wouldn't give to lay their head on the same pillows that have played host to the balding domes of prime ministers past. (With the noticeable exception of the Abbott Pillow, which still has a vague onion pong to it.) After all, it is this hallowed residence that plays host to the prime minister's preferred toilet, if there's no Macca's nearby.

But the prime minister doesn't need to just go toi-toi in Canberra, he or she may need to relieve themselves in Sydney. Hence, Kirribilli House.

Kirribilli House is the prime minister's official Sydney residence,[2] though historically

---

2   At the time of writing, the easiest way to enter the Sydney property market is by becoming Prime Minister of Australia.

its primary function has been to facilitate faux-blokesmanship between the prime minister and the Australian cricket team.

John Howard made it his primary place of residence in 1996 when he realised his Wollstonecraft home was insufficient for the task of providing an outdoor area for Warnie to sneak a ciggie. Additionally, the steep lawns are fun for kiddies to roll down, and provide good momentum when disposing of disgraced ministers into Sydney Harbour.

During his prime ministership, Malcolm Turnbull lived in his own waterfront Point Piper mansion since bunking in Kirribilli House would have been equivalent to doing the CEO Sleepout. It is believed that the main motivator for Peter Dutton to challenge for the Liberal Party leadership in 2018 was his mistaken belief that he would get to live in Turnbull's mansion. Not only did Turnbull choose to live in his own house during his prime ministership, he also chose to donate his entire parliamentary salary to charity. Plus, in the final days of the 2016 campaign, he donated more than $1 million to the Liberal Party, which then replaced him as leader two years later. Not really sure why he wanted to be prime minister, come to think of it. Probably just thought it'd look good on LinkedIn.

*

But the path to either Kirribilli House or The Lodge leads first through another house. And it's easily the most iconic, distinguished and important house in all of Australia. Yes, we are of course talking about ~~the Sydney Opera House~~ Parliament House.

Parliament House truly is 'the people's house'. Though if you do arrive with a delivery truck and start unpacking your belongings, you will be gently escorted to the people's exit. This building is the heart of our democracy. (Unless you read Australian democracy's entire Terms and Conditions, which does mention something about Buckingham Palace, but who has the time to read the whole thing?) The House contains 4700 rooms, but the three most crucial are the House of Representatives, the Senate and the Parliament House Gift Shop.

We recommend making a beeline to the gift shop first to purchase a copy of the most bloated political memoir you can find, ideally hardback. Armed with this, you'll be in a strong position to bludgeon any backbencher that attempts to get a selfie with you while inside Parliament House. The Australian Medical Association (AMA) states that even the slightest knock to the head from John Howard's 880-page *Lazarus Rising: Revised & Updated to Include the 2013 Election* can cause concussion, often leading to CTE, so do be careful. We do not recommend using the 720-page *The Menzies Era* by John Howard, as any strike dealt by a swollen prime-minister-on-prime-minister tome often kills immediately on impact. Similarly, we do not advise using *On Politics and Stuff* for bludgeoning, as even the hardiest thump from this slim volume would only result in minor irritation, through which the politician could continue their selfie-taking.

Around the parliament, you'll also often see large groups of visiting schoolchildren. For these eager minds, this is an experience they'll never forget, until the age of fourteen after they've visited some decent theme parks. Faint recollections of a portrait of Speaker Sir Littleton Groom don't stand a chance against mind-blowing memories of the Scooby-Doo Spooky Coaster at Warner Bros. Movie World. It's just a neurological fact.

Often a politician observing these schoolchildren can become lost in thought. They were once that age, the politician thinks, with all of life ahead of them. How on earth did their journey lead them to where they are now: defending policies they don't believe in, as a member of a party they've lost faith in? O, how they wish they could switch their cursed adult body with that of one of these children, forget all their woes and fuck off to Questacon to go down that slide; maybe tuck into a fun-size Cherry Ripe on the bus. Fortunately, as the *Parliamentary Handbook of the Commonwealth of Australia* (6th edition) points out, these nervous breakdowns can be easily remedied by a visit to the vending machine on level 2.

\*

The House of Representatives contains 151 seats, despite the trend for standing desks. This is where Prime Minister Kevin Rudd apologised to the Stolen Generations, with all former living prime ministers in attendance (except John Howard, who said he had something on he really couldn't get out of). It's where Prime Minister Julia Gillard delivered her iconic 'Misogyny Speech', describing Opposition Leader Tony Abbott as being a misogynist and sexist 'every day in every way'. Australians were so moved by the speech, they promptly elected Abbott prime minister less than a year later. Rhetoric in the chamber would return to the mean once Abbott began to speak exclusively in three-word slogans (e.g., 'axe the tax', 'stop the boats', 'eat the onion').

The House of Representatives' greatest claim to fame is undoubtedly as the location of *Parliament Question Time*, often considered the first reality TV show as viewers get to vote off the participants once every three years and most of the time you're watching people do nothing. The show continues to survive cancellation despite its consistently low ratings, shoddy content and revolving cast of forgettable players.

Undoubtedly, the lowest points of the show are the recurring 'Dorothy Dixer' segments, where a government backbencher asks a pre-approved, rehearsed question to a locked-and-loaded-with-talking-points government minister. These combine all the stilted acting of a pizza guy in an adult film with the sterile delivery of a Chemist Warehouse ad. And yet, much like André Rieu albums, they just keep coming. If the walls in this chamber could speak, they would probably say, 'Mr Speaker, kill me.'

Sadly, some performers stay on *Question Time* to such an age that they can no longer recall the location's official name, and just start referring to it as 'this place'. 'Some people in this place know,' they vamp, desperately looking around the chamber for any kind of signage alerting them to their current whereabouts. Those poor souls . . .

At some point during their visit, Australian primary school students will attend Question Time. This is an invaluable opportunity for schoolchildren to see what bullying looks like in a professional context. It is also the first and last time they will watch a full sitting of Question Time. We're lucky enough to have a review of Question Time from one of these primary student observers.

**Question Time report by Louie Spratt (Year 3, Baulkham Hills Primary School)**

The man standing at the desk yelled. It was a loud yell. The people behind him laughed but the people on the other side of the desk booed. The man yelling at the desk looked back at his friends behind him and they cheered more and then the people on the other side of the desk booed more. The man in the tall chair above all of them told them to be quiet but they didn't so the man in the tall chair yelled louder and they still weren't quiet and so he told the man standing at the table to get out of the green room. The man's friends cheered and the man in the tall chair told them to be quiet again, but they weren't quiet. Mr Broadhead says this is democracy and we are lucky to live in a country with this because not all countries have this. There was a large gold stick on the desk and no one picked it up and swung it around. If I was allowed to ask a question in Question Time, I think I would ask about the stick.

Thanks for that, Louie. If you're reading this book: yes, we have received your invoice, but if you read the contract again, you'll find we agreed to pay you in 'exposure'.

It is true that, to the untrained eye, Question Time can appear like one extended road rage argument without a road in sight. But it is in fact bound by strict rules which must be adhered to.[3]

---

3   For example, section 82D: 'All three female MPs must be seated within the frame of the *Question Time* cameras. No reason, there's definitely loads more ladies where they came from.'

*'It's not like just anyone can be elected
to the Senate'*

– Ricky Muir, motoring enthusiast or something like that.
What was it again? Oh, who cares . . .

There are many important differences between the Senate and the House of Representatives. Louie claims in his report that the key difference is that the House of Representatives is green and the Senate is red. After checking with multiple independent sources, the authors of this book can confirm that at the time of writing this is indeed correct, though, again, this will not result in any kind of financial compensation for Louie.

Another significant difference between the two houses – that Louie failed to touch upon in his report – is that senators are elected for six years rather than three years in the House of Reps. As a result, the seats in the Senate possess particularly formidable butt grooves. After several independent tests, the authors of this book can reveal that the craters in these seats are indeed robust. You're looking at putting in at least six months of hard arse-time to make even a slight dent.

But what do people over the age of nine think about the Senate? Well, Paul Keating famously claimed the Senate consisted of 'unrepresentative swill'. But he talks a lot of shit, doesn't he? Nevertheless, you have to admit that there is a certain low-budget stink attached to the Senate. If the House of Representatives is Netflix, the Senate is definitely Stan.[4]

Often, the balance of power in the senate comes down to a handful of crossbench senators. This can mean that sometimes the entire might of the two major parties is focused on convincing a xenophobic former *Dancing with the Stars* contestant to either support or oppose a bill. After a few dark nights of the soul and seeking counsel from different stakeholders, a crossbench senator in this position generally ends up declaring, in a tearful speech, that they

---

4    Don't get us wrong, we love Stan's catalogue and their commitment to Australian stories. But, you know . . . Also, to continue this analogy, Senate Estimates is ABC iview, and the House Standing Committees are SBS On Demand.

will be supporting the government's bill – and not just because the government has promised to deliver their constituency really fast internet and/or some kind of multimillion dollar giant Big Banana-esque novelty tourist attraction, perhaps an apricot approximately 3000 times the size of your regular-sized supermarket apricot? (No judgement please, we're just throwing out ideas here.)

At any one time, there are roughly three to five weirdos in the Senate. When the ratio of weirdos to non-weirdos gets too high, the government asks the Governor-General to flush them out with a double dissolution, the Toilet Duck of Australian electoral processes.[5]

---

5   No need to extend this analogy, it begins and ends at
    Toilet Duck.

\*

The Senate's time to really shine – if you can define shining as sitting in a stale room going over each line item in the ABC's budget – is the Senate Estimates. For most of the year, senators like Eric Abetz exist in a state of hibernation, conserving energy and surviving only on packets of Parlimints.[6]

Until finally, it's time to strike, and shame the ABC for using exorbitant amounts of taxpayers' money on their radical climate change alarmist 'emergency bushfire warnings'. Press gallery journalists love Senate Estimates because it's the one time of year

---

6   Parliament + Mints = Parlimints. Aren't you glad we
    cleared that up.

they get to use the word 'grilling'. And grilled these public servants are. How will they ever wriggle their way out of this sticky situation? What's that? Oh, they've just said they'll take the question 'on notice'. Foiled again . . .

> *'Political party infrastructure is key*
> *to electoral success'*
> – Kanye West

If you want to make it into the Senate or the House of Representatives as a politician, you'll need more than just a Murrays bus ticket. Though, a Murrays ticket is by no means a bad start (that offer code again: ONPOLITICS).

No, to make it in Canberra, you'll need to be on a *party* ticket. Unlike a Murrays ticket, which can be easily bought online or in person at a station of your choice, getting on a party ticket usually requires being 'preselected' by the party. This process varies from party to party, but it is generally designed to prevent any qualified candidates from receiving the nomination. For instance, Labor preselection is determined by which faction you're aligned to, whereas One Nation preselection is determined on a first-come, first-served basis.

The preselection process is ripe for corruption, and as such it spans the gamut of dirty tricks, from a few grubby fake signatures here and there, to good old-fashioned cash-in-envelopes-using-the-names-of-dead-people skulduggery.

But which seat should you stand for? Well, we've painstakingly copied and pasted this list of electorates from the Australian Electoral Commission (AEC) website. You're welcome.

Division of Eden-Monaro

Division of Nissan-Pajero

Division of Bendigo

Division of Uggo

Division of Corio

Division of Derro

Division of Calare

Division of Crimpy

Division of Corangamite

Division of Cheesymite

Division of iSnack2.0

Division of Longman

Division of Microwoman

Division of Herbert

Division of Bigot

Division of Capricornia

Division of Passiona

Division of McPherson

Division of McFlurry

Division of Flinders

Division of Fingers

Division of Cloudstreet

Division of Lululemon

Division of Eagleboys

Division of Country Target

Now that you've chosen your electorate, it's worth reflecting long and hard on which political party you'll join. On a whim, former Prime Minister Malcolm Turnbull chose to join the Liberal Party, a party with which he had many ideological differences. Fortunately, it ended up being a fantastic fit without any tension. But you might not be so lucky, so choose wisely.

The two major parties are the Australian Labor Party, who represent workers, and the Liberal Party who represent boat owners. These are basically the Big Mac and Quarter Pounder of Australian politics. Yeah, you could join the Filet-O-Fish. But who really cares about the Filet-O-Fish? Around 10 per cent of the Australian electorate, max?

As for how to get selected as a candidate, well, you could start by getting real-world experience outside of politics, as well as developing a genuine affinity with and understanding of the community and constituents you'd be representing. Or you could just get a shitkicker job in a minister's office picking hi-vis vests and hard hats for the minister to wear at press conferences, waiting patiently until the minister accidentally chokes to death on a dagwood dog at a school fete photo-op, sparking a by-election. It's really up to you. But if it helps, most people choose the latter. Just learn three or four things about the local area you can rattle off when handing out trophies at the Under-10s soccer awards and you'll be fine.

*

The **Australian Labor Party** was formed on 8 May 1901. On 9 May 1901, people began to complain that the Australian Labor Party was better in the old days. Out of the two major parties, the Australian Labor Party has been the party of the prime ministers who have most transformed Australia. On the other hand, they also had Mark Latham for a while, so let's not lay it on too thick.

The Labor Party is traditionally the party of 'working people', and since ALP politicians tell the media they are working for working people 20 per cent more than the Liberal Party does, that officially makes them the party for working people in Australia. In general, the Australian public views the Labor Party as stronger on healthcare, education and sculling the shit out of a beer at the cricket. Among other bad ideas, the Labor Party is famous for its factions. There are left-wing factions, right-wing factions and many sub-factions in between, but they are all united in their goal to project an image of disunity and chaos to the Australian people.

But what makes an ideal Labor Party leader?

The ideal Labor leader loves working families. In fact, the ideal Labor leader lives, eats and breathes working families.[7] The ideal Labor leader can talk to 'punters' about 'punter stuff'.[8] The ideal Labor leader can explain superannuation reform in 'punter metaphors'. The ideal Labor leader will say funny stuff occasionally, like 'Any boss who sacks anyone for not turning up today is a bum' or 'Get that interest rate cut up ya!'. The ideal Labor leader will not say 'Fair shake of the sauce

---

7    At time of writing, the Australian Medical Association
      (AMA) does not recommend ingesting or inhaling
      working families. But depends how badly you want to be
      Labor leader.

8    Footy, Bunnings, engagement in the Asia-Pacific region.

bottle' as this is a phrase generated by a deep learning Australiana AI program that is still in beta mode. The ideal Labor leader eats a sausage sandwich in a way that makes people watching them say, 'That person sure knows how to eat a sausage sandwich normally.' The ideal Labor leader is not Bill Shorten. The ideal Labor leader is a Rhodes scholar. The ideal Labor leader does not mention they are a Rhodes scholar, in case this leads punters to suspect the Labor leader is 'one of those fucken Rhodes scholars or sum shit'. Based on internal polling from the 2007 election, the ideal Labor leader has attended a strip club. The ideal Labor leader is as at home in the Bankstown RSL as they are in Buckingham Palace. The ideal Labor leader secretly prefers

Buckingham Palace. The ideal Labor leader thinks it's not even close, there's so much free food and liquor, and the bathrooms are way better, really quite schmick. The ideal Labor leader does not have any contrarian views on the South China Sea that come out of nowhere. At any given time, the ideal Labor leader knows the price of milk, the captains of both State of Origin sides and the reform agenda that can unite inner-city progressive voters and outer-suburban working-class voters. The ideal Labor leader will probably remain on the backbench.

\*

The **Liberal Party** was founded on 31 August 1945, appealing to those convinced that the 1940s had been progressive enough. Perhaps Australia's most inclusive party, the Liberal Party features people from all parts of the political spectrum, from the mildly xenophobic to the wildly bigoted. Party leaders generally fall into two camps: those who remain party lifers (John Howard, Robert Menzies) and those who distance themselves from the party post-politics (Malcolm Fraser, John Hewson, Malcolm Turnbull). Occasionally, former leaders move overseas (Tony Abbott, Harold Holt).

But what makes an ideal Liberal Party leader?

The ideal Liberal leader is poncy, but not *too* poncy. The ideal Liberal leader has a secret desire to wear a cravat but settles for a tie.

The ideal Liberal leader doesn't have a name like Ninian C. Spofforth III, just Ninian C. Spofforth III levels of entitlement. The ideal Liberal Party leader does not believe in quotas and should be chosen on 'merit', whoever he or he may be. The ideal Liberal leader has a basic name like Scott or John or ~~Julie~~ Tony. The ideal Liberal leader's wife has a glass of white glued to her hand when at home and makes withering remarks from time to time, like, 'Well, Mother never was entirely convinced you could cut the mustard, was she?' The ideal Liberal leader funnels the rage from these remarks into cruel border policies. The ideal Liberal leader promises to fight potential Labor reforms. The ideal Liberal leader promises not to undo that one completed

Labor reform. The ideal Liberal leader swears they'll stay away from that other one, too. The ideal Liberal leader likes shoes off inside the house, thank you. The ideal Liberal leader likes jam and fruit preserves far more than the average Australian but does not bring this up. The ideal Liberal leader will not, under any circumstances, fuck with Medicare, even though they want to so bad, it's all they can think about day and night and it's causing a rift in their marriage. The ideal Liberal leader will successfully hide any signs of arousal related to the mere thought of fucking with Medicare. The ideal Liberal leader lives, eats and breathes small business. The ideal Liberal leader once had their stomach pumped after attempting to consume a Blue Haven Pool.

The ideal Liberal leader is born to rule. The ideal Liberal leader was not born with any traits making them particularly suited to ruling, it's just more of a vibe . . . The ideal Liberal Party leader wants every Australian to own their own home and every investor to own multiple investment properties, and for the maths to somehow work out. The ideal Liberal Party leader's sartorial style of tie selection should range anywhere from Union Jack Blue to Blue Haven Pools blue. The ideal Liberal leader will fund that policy with a tax cut. The ideal Liberal leader hasn't got modelling on that. The ideal Liberal leader knows and loves only one *Nanette* – their great-aunt. The ideal Liberal leader will not kowtow to political correctness. The ideal Liberal leader will rent

*Breakfast at Tiffany's* on iTunes and think Mickey Rooney's performance was 'a delight'. The ideal Liberal leader won't be on board with observing people's preferred gender pronouns. The ideal Liberal leader will be fine with calling a grown man 'Twiggy'. The ideal Liberal Party leader is not photographed eating, lest the Australian public witness them polishing off a Chips on a Stick with a knife and fork. The ideal Liberal Party leader should openly express their frustration with the hard right of the Liberal Party, preferably years after they've left office, when it will make fuck-all difference. The ideal Liberal leader will become prime minister. For *aaaages*.

*

If you prefer a party that represents 'real' Australians (i.e., cattle), you could always try the **Nationals**. The Nationals are the Liberal Party but with Akubras. The party represents regional Australia, so to qualify as a member you must submit your tractor licence and R.M. Williams loyalty card number. The Nationals are in a coalition with the Liberal Party, an agreement from which they receive many benefits. Offhand, none come to mind, but the party's leader gets to sit next to the prime minister sometimes. As for the Liberal Party, the benefits of the agreement with the National Party are many, though primarily it serves to make the Liberals' homophobes, racists and religious zealots seem woke by comparison.

When a Liberal prime minister goes on holiday, the Nationals leader becomes 'Acting PM', the political equivalent of the fill-in news presenters you see during the summer holidays – you can't remember their names, but they were fine, I guess? There's a saying in show business that you should 'never take a holiday' because your replacement could end up doing a better job than you. No Liberal prime minister has ever had such concerns; they take holidays all the time.

It is occasionally an uneasy relationship due to the differing priorities of the two parties (one desires 'small government', the other 'big hats'). The Liberal–National Coalition exists in all states and territories except in one state where the parties have merged as the LNP.

I wonder which Australian state could possibly be so contrarian.[9]

\*

The **Greens** were formed in 1992 as a party for Labor Party members who can't stand the idea of ever being in government. A pragmatic party, in 2009 the Greens voted down the carbon emissions trading scheme after fearing supporting the bill could alienate their climate change sceptic base. Unlike most political parties, the Greens actually believe in things, leading most Australians to conclude they're insufferable. Sadly, most Greens parliamentarians go on to develop a unique

---

9    It's Queensland. Of course it's Queensland. Why did you even look down here?

form of tinnitus, where the sound ringing in their ears is 'That's all well and good, but how are you gonna pay for it?'

Pauline Hanson is a federal senator, unfortunately. She founded the **One Nation Party** in 1997, after being disendorsed by the Liberal Party – for either being too racist or not racist enough, can't recall. Recognising the potential threat and harm that Hanson's views could cause, the Australian media welcomed her on to their programs to expand on them further. Every election, One Nation candidates compete to see who can come up with the most creative way to disgrace themselves. In 2017, one candidate resigned after a photo emerged showing him saluting a swastika he'd mowed into his lawn. Say what you will about the awful incident, you can't deny it's unique.

The **Bullet Train for Australia Party** was not so much a party as it was a movement. A really fast movement from Melbourne to Newcastle, with brief stops in Canberra and Sydney. Though deregistered in 2017, the Bullet Train for Australia Party lives on in the hearts, minds and dreams of Australians from all walks of life, be they rail track inspectors, signal operators or assistant rail track inspectors.

There are also usually one or two **Independents**. They refuse to be affiliated with any political party because they're still trying to come up with a name for their own one. They know they want their name in there, but what are they, a team? A network? These are the decisions that keep the Independent up at night.

*'Leaders aren't born, they're made'*

– Instagram post (can't remember which account, sorry)

For those who do go on to lead an Australian political party, it will be the honour of their lifetime. An honour they'll reflect on for years to come. Often late at night, in a clammy sweat, wondering how it all went so fucking wrong.

But, of course, the real goal is to become prime minister. And who wouldn't want to be prime minister? It's no exaggeration to say that every Australian child dreams of the day when they can be booed by the crowd at the NRL Grand Final.

There are many ways to get the gig. Yes, you could win an election, but that sounds like an awful lot of work. Personally, we recommend the John McEwen approach of just waiting around until the PM decides not to swim between the flags. The most popular method, however, is the democratically robust system of 'knifing'. At the time of writing, only one of the last five changes of prime minister occurred through an actual election, and that was when Tony Abbott was elected to the office. So maybe democracy's not all it's cracked up to be.

It's been said that the Australian cricket captain is the most important position in the country after the prime minister, when in fact the prime minister doesn't even rank in the top ten.[10]

At the time of writing, Australia has only had one female prime minister. If you discount the tsunami of sexism, the threats that she should be thrown out to sea in a chaff bag and the fact that a man stole the role from her midway through her term, it went really

---

10
10. Chief Justice of the High Court
9. Late-night kebab shop owner
8. Hemsworth brother
7. Face of AAMI
6. Hot barista
5. Intern inside the *Sunrise* Cash Cow
4. Guardian of the Nation's Chicken Salt Supply
3. Video referee
2. Bunnings Sausage Sizzle operator
1. Sam Neill
SOURCE: Australian Bureau of Statistics report, 'Australia at a Glance: The Ten Most Important Positions in the Nation'.

well. Unfortunately, many Australians weren't ready for a female prime minister as, at that point, they'd only experienced sixty years of a female head of state. Fortunately, the Australian media seamlessly adapted to having a female prime minister, asking the same questions about clothing choices, butt size and their spouse's occupation they would have asked of any male prime minister.

Nevertheless, it would have been hard to even imagine a female prime minister back in 1943, when Dame Enid Lyons became the first woman to serve in the House of Representatives. After Enid's husband, Prime Minister Joseph Lyons, died in office, she went into politics herself. More than you can say for Mary Todd Lincoln. Lyons had twelve children, served in Cabinet, sat on the board of the ABC, wrote a popular newspaper column, and had the technology existed at the time, would have had a decent podcast.

Holding the prime minister to account is the opposition leader. Being opposition leader in Australia is a tough job, though if you compare it to being opposition leader in Russia, it's a piece of piss. Occasionally an opposition leader attempts to present a bold reform agenda. The dangers of this approach could be observed when Opposition Leader John Hewson stumbled while explaining the proposed GST during the infamous 'birthday cake interview', subsequently losing the 'unlosable' election. To this day, he's a fucking mess if he passes a Michel's Patisserie.

*'It must be said that above all, there is no more important quality for a leader to possess than empathy. Without it, any leadership would surely be impossible'*
– Tup Leach, Bullet Train for Australia Party

*'We have nothing to fear but those little fish in the Amazon that swim up your peehole'*
– Franklin D. Roosevelt, 1933 inaugural address (first draft)

Deciding what type of leader one should become is one of the hardest decisions one can make. Thankfully, you don't really have a choice in the matter; whatever personality flaws you have developed will inevitably be revealed when you threaten to shirtfront a dictator. Nevertheless, if you would like some inspiration for who you might attempt to model your leadership style after, here are some of the most in-depth, nuanced biographies of Australian leaders ever written.

*

After leading a life consisting of no memorable achievements other than becoming Australia's first prime minister, **Edmund Barton** is today perhaps best remembered for becoming Australia's first prime minister. Barton's influence can still be felt today, particularly in trivia questions like: 'Who was Australia's first prime minister?'

*

**Robert Menzies** was Australia's longest serving prime minister, holding the position for a period many historians have described as 'taking the piss'. He was the founder of the Liberal Party, choosing the name based on his approach to economic and social policy, and because 'The Sex Party' was already taken. He won an incredible seven consecutive elections, narrowly outnumbering Kim Beazley's election victories by seven.

\*

At time of writing, **John Howard** is Australia's oldest living prime minister, unless you're still out there, Harold. Known to dress up as Robert Menzies at cosplay events, he is best remembered for throwing asylum-seeking children overboard (citation needed). Howard refused to apologise to the Stolen Generations during his time in office, but to be fair to him, he also failed to turn up for the apology years later. Howard stated that he 'did not subscribe to the black armband view of history'.[11]

He introduced the gun buyback scheme in 1996 and now has Australia's largest collection of guns. During a 2010 appearance on *Q&A*, an audience member threw shoes at the former PM, finally giving him justification for wearing that bulletproof vest. Though opinions are divided on his legacy, he is

---

11  The black armband view of history is the idea
    that Australia's history books should highlight the
    mistreatment of Indigenous Australians instead of
    outlining the fine batting record of one Sir Donald
    Bradman.

universally praised for ensuring Mark Latham did not become prime minister.

\*

**Tony Abbott** was Australia's 28th prime minister and he ate a fucking onion. He campaigned on policies of stopping the boats, axing the tax and he put the whole fucking onion in his mouth. An avid cyclist and runner, he put a raw onion that hadn't even been washed into his mouth and ingested a large amount of it. A climate change sceptic, he shut down the Climate Commission and then didn't even seem to react to the fact that he was chewing on onion skin. He will be remembered for picking up a raw onion, looking at the raw onion and actually fucking eating the raw onion.

\*

Labor Prime Minister **Bob Hawke** was many things: a Rhodes scholar, trade unionist and bold economic reformer, but all Australians agree his defining legacy is drinking a beer really fast at the cricket a few times. Hawke had a turbulent personal life, at one point marrying his biographer, having failed to read that clause in the contract with Schwartz Publishing. As prime minister, he reinstated Medicare, replacing the existing 'kiss it better' health system. He also changed the national anthem from 'God Save the Queen' to 'Shaddap You Face' (Dolce, Joe, Full Moon Records) and then, following a backlash, to 'Advance Australia Fair'.

\*

**Paul Keating** was Australia's best prime minister and best treasurer.[12]

Keating didn't fit the mould of a typical Labor leader as he didn't seem to have ever watched or participated in the kicking of a ball. During the Hawke–Keating years, he laid the foundation for his future work: defending the legacy of the Hawke–Keating years. As treasurer, one of his most notable achievements was 'floating the dollar'. Far from being some kind of mind-blowing David Blaine-esque magic trick with a dollar note, it's actually a pretty dry economic reform. Wouldn't bother googling it, to be honest.

---

12  SOURCE: Keating, Paul.

Keating dedicated his 1993 election victory to 'the true believers', a large group of Australians who deeply believed in the cause of the Labor Party and who became extinct around mid-2008. To this day, if you say the phrase 'changes to superannuation' three times into a mirror, Paul Keating will appear and eviscerate you.

\*

Born in 1957, **Kevin Rudd** was raised on a dairy farm in rural Queensland, a point he would bring up many times to hide the fact that he was actually raised inside a filing cabinet in a minister's office. In 2007, Kevin07's campaign for prime minister looked like it might be going off the rails when it was revealed he had visited a strip club while representing Australia in New York. The public forgave him though, when they realised this was probably the first time he'd seen a naked lady.

On 13 February 2008, Prime Minister Kevin08 delivered an apology to the Stolen Generations, so at least he got that right. He garnered an abundance of public sympathy after losing the leadership to Julia Gillard in 2010, but he squandered that when he decided to do his interviews on *The Killing Season* in a 'funny' persona he calls 'Hannibal Ruddster'.

Kevin Rudd returned to the prime ministership in 2013, but like that *Murphy Brown* reboot, it just didn't really work. He was brought back to 'save the furniture' and since growing a beard, he looks like he's been sleeping on a couch.

*

From 1996 to 2012, **Bob Brown** was the leader of the Australian Greens, leading the party out of the wilderness and then, for environmentally conscious reasons, back into the wilderness. Brown hasn't been involved in federal politics since 2012 but he's still the first name most people think of when you say 'the Greens'; he's like the Greens equivalent of Andrew Gaze. His work has saved more greenery than Jim's Mowing has mowed down, which is a lot of greenery.

There are differing accounts of Bob Brown's childhood. Brown says that he was raised in Sydney's western suburbs and graduated from the University of Sydney with a degree in medicine. The *Daily Telegraph* says he spent his formative years on a communal marijuana farm doing yoga and socialism.

Bob Brown joined the Liberal Party in his twenties before representing the Greens in the Senate in his fifties, a trajectory political scientists have labelled 'weird'. He was the first openly gay member of the Australian parliament, which must have been a breeze. He currently lives with his partner in Eggs and Bacon Bay[13] in Tasmania, which sounds awful.

After chaining himself to the publisher's desk at Hardie Grant, Brown was permitted

---

13 That's no joke, it's really called Eggs and Bacon Bay. And it looks horrendously idyllic.

to release his memoir, *Optimism*, in 2014, and you'd better believe that was printed on recycled paper. Brown has remained a lifelong campaigner for Tasmania's wilderness, which, until Mona was built, accounted for 100 per cent of the state.

*

As prime minister, **Malcolm Fraser** accepted tens of thousands of refugees fleeing Vietnam, a decision that has helped Australia become the vibrant, thriving multicultural nation it is today. He also once wandered into the foyer of a Memphis hotel wearing only his underpants so, all in all, a bit of a mixed bag.

In 1977, he established the Special Broadcasting Service (SBS) so he could find out what other countries were saying about him. As for the foreign films featuring genitalia, that was pure cream. In 2009, Malcolm Fraser ended his Liberal Party membership, citing political differences and too many emails.

\*

**Julia Gillard**, or 'Joo-liar' as she liked to be known, was Australia's first female prime minister. Many experts suggested she should have been thrown out to sea in a chaff bag.[14]

\*

**Mark Latham** was the leader of the Australian Labor Party from 2003 to 2005 and joined

---

14  Guest contributor, Alan Jones.

Pauline Hanson's One Nation Party in 2018, a trajectory political scientists have labelled 'fuckin' weird'. Latham famously crushed John Howard's hand in one of the Seven Great Feats required to become prime minister. He failed the other six.

*

Everyone who met **Gough Whitlam** feels a special affinity with him, but the reality is he only called them 'comrade' because he couldn't remember their name. He won the 1972 election partly based on his bold reform agenda, partly because William McMahon's slogan 'It's William McMahon O'Clock' simply couldn't compete with Gough Whitlam's much simpler 'It's Time'.

The Whitlam Government unravelled the way most governments do: attempting to borrow US$4 billion from an obscure Pakistani financial broker. But to be fair to the government, that guy was offering better interest rates than the NAB. Governor-General Sir John Kerr removed Whitlam partly due to this scandal, but mainly because he couldn't get the 'It's Time' song out of his head.

So beloved was Whitlam, the architect of Medicare and free university, that following 'the dismissal', he only went on to lose two consecutive elections.

\*

Despite the period from 2007 to 2018 when there was a concerted effort to ensure as many people got to be prime minister as possible, most of the folks elected to public office will never get to the top job. Fortunately, there is a series of runner-up prizes that will look nice on your CV when applying for board appointments post-politics.

The most coveted Cabinet position is treasurer because it's the only role that comes with its own guaranteed prime-time TV special. On one Tuesday each year, the ABC's 7.30 pm slot is dedicated to the treasurer's budget speech, relegating Leigh Sales to the graveyard shift of 8 pm.

The communications minister is responsible for ensuring that Australians have access to the best technology available fifteen years ago, while the immigration portfolio is usually given to the MP who's okay with not sleeping at night. Knowledge of the UN Refugee Convention not necessary.

The education minister is responsible for commissioning studies into alternate funding models for Australia's educational institutions and then not following through on any of the recommendations. The education minister may often find themselves embroiled in the 'history wars' over the structure of Australia's curriculum. (Australia's current history curriculum mix: one-fifth Indigenous history, one-fifth British history, three-fifths a VHS of Peter Weir's *Gallipoli*.)

The minister for agriculture is required to visit country areas and assure farmers that the government will make it rain more this year.

Traditionally, the minister will say they can't hear that question about coal seam gas over the sound of a tractor.

The environment minister is responsible for ensuring that Australia's environment remains free from interference from environmentalists and is returned to its rightful owners: the top bidder.

*'Nice bus, good condition, 100,000 km,*
*has Bill Shorten's face on the side'*
– Gumtree ad

For politicians, the campaign trail is a gruelling weeks-long process where thousands of hours of engaging with the Australian public about their needs and concerns gets condensed to a few seconds of news footage of you tripping on a doorstep or eating a pie a bit weird.

Long after their political careers have ended, some politicians are still remembered for the gaffes they made on the campaign trail: when Tony Abbott referred to himself as the suppository of all wisdom; the time John Howard accidentally referred to the Queen as 'Mum'; when Nick Xenophon's prop 'pork barrel' rolled down a hill and into a nearby synagogue and when Tony Abbott visited the Big Pineapple and bit straight into it.

The cliché of the campaign trail is that candidates go around 'kissing babies', when the reality, of course, is that most of the campaign is spent tongue-kissing seniors. For voters, however, the experience of the campaign will vary depending on whether you live in a 'safe' or 'marginal' seat. If you're not clear if you live in a safe seat, the easy way to work it out is that safe Liberal seats are ones where residents own leafblowers, while safe Labor seats are ones where you can walk down the street without a shirt on.

Although living in a safe seat means your vote won't matter, the upside is it also means you will most likely not see any politician in the flesh, as they have nothing to gain from speaking to you. Sadly, if you live in a marginal electorate, it means you are one of the few thousand Australians who will decide the outcome of this democratic process millions of people participate in, and as such, you will see politicians approximately three to five times a day.

We recommend avoiding shopping at supermarkets in case you are cornered by one and buying clothing with extra pockets for the additional leaflets that will be thrust upon you during this campaign. We don't wish to alarm you, but because of your location, there is the possibility that some politicians may even knock on your door to discuss their policies. While you are forbidden by law from inflicting violence on a politician knocking on your door, according to Section 72C of the *Australian Electoral Commission Guidebook*, you are permitted to chase them off with a broom.

*'Democracy can, from time to time, cast peculiar spells on citizens, resulting in the exhibiting of a wide range of strange behaviours. Though one can think these behaviours inessential and inconvenient, one finds they may be just as essential to a democracy's smooth functioning as the ballot box or the free press. That being said, I just don't really get "the worm"'*

– Alexis de Tocqueville, *Democracy in Australia*

Politics is a contest of ideas, and when it comes to televised debates, the winner of the contest is determined by a worm. Not a literal worm. Not like that octopus that determined the 2010 World Cup, sadly, but an on-screen squiggle which depicts voters' changing moods as they listen to the candidates for the first time. The Australian public watches politics with a sharp eye and will not hesitate to discard a government if the newspaper with the most footy coverage tells them to.

*

Election day is the triennial highlight of the political calendar when the Australian public gets to determine who will be the next prime minister to be rolled by their own party room. While it is an opportunity to exercise one's democratic right, it is first and foremost a bake sale. Much has been made of the so-called 'democracy sausage', but this tends to overshadow the gravity of the day and, more importantly, the crucial role of the 'democracy lamington' and the lesser known 'democracy snot block'.[15]

Voting was made compulsory in Australia in 1924, after politicians discovered that voters were just eating the sausage sandwich then heading home. The process itself takes place primarily in school halls around the country, so that big feeling you get of carrying out your democratic duty is actually a reflection of the fact that the school really is smaller than you remember. It is true that many voters do not make up their mind about who to vote for until they reach the polling place, giving them only a few minutes to peruse the pamphlets thrust into them upon arrival. Unfortunately, this crucial cramming period is usually spent

---

15  Only available in Victoria.

brushing up on the names of the various school captains[16] on the wall.

'Informal voting' is the name given to the proud Australian tradition of expressing your dissatisfaction with the candidates through an artistic imprint on the ballot paper,[17] or indeed any vote that does not adhere to the tyrannical, numbers-based approach to voting.

'Informal voting' is also known as a 'protest vote', so as AEC officials are asking 'if you'll be much longer' while you're on your third attempt of the dorsal vein, remember, you're basically Gandhi right now.

---

16 Sadly, as much as 90 per cent of the One Nation vote is attributed to last-minute decisions by voters observing that the names of the school captains have, in recent years, 'gotten a bit Asian'.

17 Traditionally, a cartoon dick and balls.

Although the rate of informal voting is only about 6 per cent – and always effing hilarious – the practice must be exercised with some caution as a high rate of informal votes resulted in an actual dick and balls being elected to the seat of Werriwa in 1994.[18]

It is the authors' hope that as the representation of women in Australian parliament increases, so too will the depiction of female genitalia on Australian ballot papers. That's right, we're feminists.

Regardless of where you live, the choice of candidates is more or less the same:

---

18  Electoral results for the seat of Werriwa, 1994:
LYNN, Charlie (Liberal) 20,4666 votes
LATHAM, Mark William (Labor) 30,337 votes

Family man (homophobe/adulterer)

Thoroughly decent community member
(hopeless Independent)

Incumbent who will die in this seat
(Liberal Party)

Candidate who looks normal in
Birkenstocks (Greens Party)

Soon-to-be disgraced trade unionist
(Labor Party)

Larrikin, outspoken local bloke (racist)

Once you've cast your vote, all that's left to do is to go home and watch footage on television of the prime minister and opposition leader submitting their votes with their families and conclude that you did a better job. It's been a long day. Time to gently nod off to the sound of the ABC's psephologist, Antony Green, aggressively poking his touch screen like a sociopathic kid with a dead frog.

*

For the unsuccessful candidate in the race, your concession speech will be a chance to acknowledge the 'lessons learned'[19] from this campaign. You won't have to actually apply these lessons, though, as this is the last speech you'll ever give. As for the successful candidate, your speaking days are just beginning as being a parliamentarian means you'll be expected to speak at community events, memorials, and the occasional far-right rally that you had

---

19  Don't use the c-word in an argument at retirement home bingo next campaign.

'no idea' was a far-right rally. As such, you'll want to hire a speechwriter, someone who understands your voice, who can expand upon your ideas and whose contributions you'll be quick to downplay when they really nail that one about reconciliation.

Your first speech in parliament will be referred to as your 'maiden speech', and at latest estimates, we've got two to three years before that term becomes problematic. In this speech, you'll want to thank your family in the viewing gallery. Get a good look at them, because this is the last time you'll see them until you leave office.

Twitter, Facebook, Instagram . . . all of these are exciting opportunities for you to engage with your constituents and for them to call you a Nazi. Once in office, you'll want to employ someone with no understanding of social media as your social media manager. This person will be responsible for posting poorly filmed videos with bad sound and creating stale memes for the online masses to pillory. It will also be this person's job to go through your old problematic social media posts and leave them up there for everyone to find. Hope you enjoyed that 'Come as a famous figure from the 1940s' fancy-dress party when you were twenty-two, you're going to be hearing a lot about it.

But while you can control your message through your tweets, TikToks and, inevitably, OnlyFans content, one thing you can't control is the media.

\*

The Australian media landscape is vibrant, vast and largely owned by a man named Rupert. Rupert came to own the Australian media landscape through a mixture of hard work, determination and his dad dying. Rupert pursues aggressive tax minimisation strategies in Australia. This is understandable, as Rupert prefers to give back to the nation in other ways, primarily by providing employment for a certain kind of troubled individual who wouldn't find a job elsewhere: the Conservative Commentator.

No one is better equipped to speak for suburban Australia than the Conservative Commentator. (After all, they lived in the suburbs for seven whole years while they went to private boarding school.) The Conservative Commentator is infuriated by dole bludgers. These people are stealing our hard-earned tax dollars by accepting their Disability Support Pension, when the Conservative Commentator is pretty sure they're not *that* disabled. The Conservative Commentator firmly believes anyone who cheats taxpayers is scum. (Their employer excluded, of course.) And for the Conservative Commentator, there is no bigger cheater of taxpayers than the ABC. Day after day, the Conservative Commentator will try to distort the Australian public's perception to the point where their readers begin to believe the corporation's $1 billion annual budget is spent on one giant soy latte, in which the out-of-touch, inner-city presenters frolic and wash their private parts at taxpayers' expense. The only time the Conservative Commentator listens to the ABC is for the emergency broadcasts during bushfires, and, even then, it could be categorised as a 'hate-listen'.

*

Achieving office in Australia is a grave responsibility which not only requires you to represent the Australians who voted for you, but also to say in your victory speech that you will represent the Australians who didn't vote for you.[20]

Many bemoan the state of divisiveness and lack of compromise in Australian politics, but

---

20  You don't actually have to represent them; the speech is more than enough.

it wasn't always this way. During World War I, Prime Minister Joseph Cook and Opposition Leader Andrew Fisher both pledged support for the British war effort. By the end of the war, with 60,000 Australians dead, it was decided that Australian prime ministers and opposition leaders should never agree on anything ever again.

The general approach to governing in Australia is to construct a bold reform agenda and then become distracted by whatever crisis comes up that week. Key thing to remember: a bill must pass through both houses before it becomes law.[21]

A renewable energy bill is slightly different, however, as it must go through a process of

---

21  Thanks for letting us know that, Louie.

watering down and, ultimately, abandonment. Other than that, it's exactly the same.

If a treasurer delivers a budget deficit, they are considered a failure. It doesn't matter if they saved Australia from the Global Financial Crisis, a budget deficit is a sign of economic mismanagement.[22]

But what else do we know about governing? To be honest, that's basically it. We know someone once said, 'Laws are like sausages', but we can't remember the rest of the aphorism, or who uttered it. Best guess is either Otto von Bismarck or Iain 'Huey' Hewitson.[23]

---

22 The Liberal Party excluded. You're doing a great job!

23 Hewitson, Iain. Restaurateur, chef, television personality, former face of the supermarket chain BI-LO. Bismarck, Otto von. Politics dude.

In all seriousness, as Australian citizens who care about the future of our political system, we advise aspiring leaders to seek governing advice from these excellent books from the On Series:

Paul Keating's *On ~~Hawke~~ Me*

John Howard's *On a Morning Walk, Will be Back in Ten Minutes*

Kevin Rudd's *On Denial, On Anger, On Bargaining, On Depression, On Acceptance, On Handball*

Julia Gillard's *On Tony*

Malcolm Turnbull's *On Tony*

Tony Abbott's *'Skin On': A New Approach to an Old Vegetable*

Scott Morrison's *On QF3 to Honolulu*

*'What's next for me after I leave Parliament? Well, I'll tell you one thing, I'm definitely not starting my own podcast'*
– Christopher Pyne, host of *Pyne Time*, available on Spotify, Whooshkaa and Apple Podcasts

There are two ways to leave Canberra: in a Murrays coach or in disgrace. (We know which one we'd prefer. . . Go on, tell them Mark and Evan sent you and you'll receive a complimentary shrug of indifference.) There are many reasons to leave a life in politics but the template resignation letter already has 'spend more time with my family' pre-loaded, so just go with that. On the plus side, when God closes a door, he opens a window to a lobbying firm and, in extreme cases, the Sky News studio.

Oh, we almost forgot, there is a final way to leave Canberra: in a hearse (not Murrays). Although your cadaver won't enjoy the style and comfort it's been accustomed to under the team at Murrays, on the plus side, you will receive a state funeral attended by everyone you ever hated.

Bob Hawke famously declared, 'By 1990, no Australian child will be living in poverty.' Although we've fallen short of that particular target, it is true that no Australian child is living without a political memoir. The most recent census found that there were

3.7 political memoirs for every Australian, and it's predicted that by 2030, political memoirs will outnumber Australians by a ratio of 10:1. Of course, not every politician writes a book after they leave parliament. Some of them write one while they're still in it.[24]

If you're a former prime minister, you have an open invitation to be interviewed on the ABC's *7.30* whether you've got a book out or you've just seen something in the news that's rubbed you the wrong way. For everyone else, *The Drum* will be in touch once the Howard-era guests start to die off.

---

24  See: Chris Bowen's *The Money Men: Australia's Twelve Most Notable Treasurers,* Cory Bernardi's *The Conservative Revolution* and Tony Abbott's *Five-Second Meals: From Paddock to Gob.*

## Afterword

As we await our departure[25] from Canberra's Jolimont Centre in our neutral-scented, air-conditioned transport – just one of the seventy new coaches purchased by Murrays in recent years that has rightly earned Murrays the title of the operator of Australia's largest modern coach fleet – we

---

25  To be clear, the delayed departure was no fault of the team at Murrays but was instead due to a customer visiting from Queensland who had failed to understand the start of DST and had called ahead to say they would be ten minutes late. After a show of hands, all aboard agreed to wait for our no doubt sleep-deprived fellow traveller. That's the Murrays difference.

can't help but reflect on the torchbearers for Australia's democracy, rated by TripAdvisor users as one of the top ten democracies in the Southern Hemisphere.

Theodore Roosevelt once said, 'It is not the critic who counts; not the man who points out how the strong man stumbles, or where the doer of deeds could have done them better. The credit belongs to the man who is actually in the arena, whose face is marred by dust and sweat and blood. . .' Anyway, kinda goes on like that for a while, but we think the gist of what he's saying is that the people who enter politics – even if they fail miserably – matter more than the people who shit on them through prose. Yeah, what a prick, right? Exactly what we were thinking too.

Nevertheless, we have to acknowledge that the amount of times this quote has been turned into some kind of graphic for social media means there might be some truth in what Roosevelt says. If it were not for the brave men <u>or women</u> (see, we're better than Roosevelt on that front) in the arena, maybe the fabric of our democracy might never have been sown, having all kinds of nightmarish consequences. If it were not for the brave soul, face marred by dust and sweat and blood, eating a raw onion, would it be possible for two writers to pen what many critics will hail as 'a frankly disproportionate number' of quips about a politician eating a raw onion? This we do not know. All we do know, dear reader, is this.

Choose Murrays.

*Acknowledgements*

It was a privilege to write this book, the definitive history of Australian politics. It is absolutely possible to acknowledge by name everyone who helped us with this book, but we choose not to for stylistic reasons. We remain in the debt of numerous individuals, all of whom work at Commonwealth Bank and will never track us down, no matter how hard they try. We remind them that for rights purposes, this book was written and published in the Cayman Islands.

In all seriousness, thank you to Barrie Cassidy for his advice. We learnt so much from his email auto-reply. We hope your break is going well, Barrie. This acknowledgement section would not be complete without thanking Don Watson for his forbearance. We don't know what forbearance means, and hopefully we will never have to find out. For their help, kindness, patience and unfailing generosity, we thank the Australian politics Wikipedia page.

To our beloved families, whose names will come to us, thank you for your incisive questions like 'How's the book going?' and 'Does that actually count as a "book"?'

Above all, our thanks go to McPherson's Printing Group, with particular thanks to the Kolbus KM 600 high-speed binder. Couldn't have done it without you, mate.

# ACKNOWLEDGEMENTS

Finally, thank you to this Acknowledgements section for its invaluable assistance in reaching our contractual word count.